Elizabeth
TO

Mom & Dad
FROM

December 25, 1999
DATE

LITTLE ONES

C O L L E C T I O N

LITTLE HUGS FOR YOU

Photography © 1998 by Virginia Dixon

Text copyright © 1998 by Garborg's, Inc.

Design by Thurber Creative

Published by Garborg's, Inc.
P. O. Box 20132, Bloomington, MN 55420

Scripture quotations marked NIV are taken from the
HOLY BIBLE, NEW INTERNATIONAL VERSION® NIV®.
Copyright © 1973, 1978, 1984 by International Bible Society.
Used by permission of Zondervan Publishing House.

Scripture quotations marked TLB are taken from
The Living Bible, Copyright © 1971. Used by permission
of Tyndale House Publishers, Inc., Wheaton, IL 60189.
All rights reserved.

ISBN 1-881830-748

Printed in Hong Kong

Little Hugs
for You

Everyone was meant to share
God's all-abiding love and care;
He saw that we would need to know
a way to let these feelings show....
So God made hugs.

JILL WOLF

Friends warm the world
with happiness.

Our lives are filled with simple joys
and blessings without end
And one of the greatest joys in life
is to have a friend.

Some people make the world special
just by being in it.

A true
friend
is always
loyal.

PROVERBS 17:17 TLB

Perhaps you'd be a bit surprised
how often, if you knew,
A joke, a song, a memory
will make me think of you.

The more I know you, the more
I want to know you more.

ROY LESSIN

Laughter is the shortest distance
between two people.

VICTOR BORGE

The happiness of life is made up
of little things—a smile, a hug,
a moment of shared laughter.

Friendship
is a hug
just when
you need it.

Knowing what to say
is not always necessary;
just the presence of
a caring friend can
make a world of
difference.

SHERI CURRY

Friendship is not
created by what we give,
but more by what we
share. It makes a
whole world of things
easier to bear.

Thoughtfulness is to friendship
what sunshine is to a garden.

May you be given more
and more of God's kindness,
peace, and love.

JUDE 1:2 TLB

In friendship's fragrant garden,
There are flowers of every hue.
Each with its own fair beauty
And its gift of joy for you.

A friend is what the heart
needs all the time.

HENRY VAN DYKE

Don't walk in front of me,
I may not follow.
Don't walk behind me,
I may not lead.
Walk beside me and
just be my friend.

ALBERT CAMUS

I'm so glad you are here....
It helps me to realize how
beautiful my world is.

RAINER MARIA RILKE

May the Lord of peace himself
give you peace at all times
and in every way.

2 THESSALONIANS 3:16 NIV

To be able to find joy in another's joy,
that is the secret of happiness.

GEORGE BERNANOS

A loving heart will always
know the feelings words
can't always show.

You are a blessing sent
from Heaven above,
a huggable reminder
of God's unfailing love.

Blessed is the
influence of one
true, loving soul
on another.

GEORGE ELIOT

Favorite people, favorite places,
favorite memories of the past...
These are the joys of a lifetime...
These are the things that last.